BOA
EDITIONS LTD

A Cluster of Noisy Planets

A Cluster of Noisy Planets

prose poems by

Charles Rafferty

AMERICAN POETS CONTINUUM SERIES, No. 190

BOA EDITIONS, LTD.　❧　ROCHESTER, NY　❧　2021

First Edition
21 22 23 24 7 6 5 4 3 2 1

For information about permission to reuse any material from this book, please contact The Permissions Company at www.permissionscompany.com or e-mail permdude@gmail.com.

Publications by BOA Editions, Ltd.—a not-for-profit corporation under section 501 (c) (3) of the United States Internal Revenue Code—are made possible with funds from a variety of sources, including public funds from the Literature Program of the National Endowment for the Arts; the New York State Council on the Arts, a state agency; and the County of Monroe, NY. Private funding sources include the Max and Marian Farash Charitable Foundation; the Mary S. Mulligan Charitable Trust; the Rochester Area Community Foundation; the Ames-Amzalak Memorial Trust in memory of Henry Ames, Semon Amzalak, and Dan Amzalak; the LGBT Fund of Greater Rochester; and contributions from many individuals nationwide. See Colophon on page 80 for special individual acknowledgments.

Cover Art: "Take Two: Once in a Blue Moon" by Pat Pauly
Cover Design: Daphne Morrissey
Interior Design and Composition: Richard Foerster
BOA Logo: Mirko

BOA Editions books are available electronically through BookShare, an online distributor offering Large-Print, Braille, Multimedia Audio Book, and Dyslexic formats, as well as through e-readers that feature text to speech capabilities.

Library of Congress Cataloging-in-Publication Data

Names: Rafferty, Charles, 1965- author.
Title: A cluster of noisy planets : prose poems / by Charles Rafferty.
Description: First Edition. | Rochester, NY : BOA Editions, Ltd., 2021. |
  Series: American poets continuum series ; no. 190 |
Identifiers: LCCN 2021009565 (print) | LCCN 2021009566 (ebook) | ISBN
  9781950774470 (paperback) | ISBN 9781950774487 (ebook)
Subjects: LCGFT: Poetry.
Classification: LCC PS3568.A378 C58 2021 (print) | LCC PS3568.A378
  (ebook) | DDC 811/.54—dc23
LC record available at https://lccn.loc.gov/2021009565
LC ebook record available at https://lccn.loc.gov/2021009566

BOA Editions, Ltd.
250 North Goodman Street, Suite 306
Rochester, NY 14607
www.boaeditions.org
A. Poulin, Jr., Founder (1938–1996)

Contents

For Wendy, Callan, and Chatham

Greetings

I counted the water towers, the active smokestacks. These were the breadcrumbs I thought would lead me back. Now I know it's possible to drive so far we forget why we left, that the journey continues even after the car breaks down. I used to think I had no message, but the message is me—bloodshot and hungry, spilled coffee down the front of my shirt. People of the future, gather round. I have traveled through ink to greet you.

The Pond

The world is in short supply. This field of goldenrod will never be enough, and the ocean feels suddenly crossable. In every apple an orchard waits, but who has 20 years to cultivate it? Above our house, the contrails of the jets have turned into actual clouds. The rain they promise is another lie. Meanwhile, the taste of my blood implies that I am rusting, that a broken machine lies half-submerged in the pond I carry with me.

A River of Birds

A river of birds filled the sky above his house. It went on for days. That many animals can't be wrong, he reasoned, as he waited for the frost to blossom. He thought about his prospects: a half tank of gas, the cabinets full of soup. Later, when the river went dry, he endured its blue and empty channel. The birds that remained were different. They shook once against the cold. They sat on the wires and looked down on him, undeterred by the lack of bounty.

Marbles

At a certain point "manic depression" became "bipolar disorder." The world has always been in flux. Just look at the sky. There are fewer stars now than when I was a boy. I cannot say who took them, I cannot remember the pictures that they made. Consider Istanbul. It used to be Constantinople, and before that Byzantium. Nothing endures. I had a jaw men wanted to punch. Now the ground I stand upon feels like it's made of marbles. In Wyoming, they've just begun hunting the grizzly bear again. It is finally safe enough to be killed. I can't get over it. My teeth were once a dazzling white, all three of my brothers were living.

The Roman Names

Zeus became Jupiter and so forth. That was the first diminishment. Then Christianity seeped in and cracked the boulder of Rome. When you lose territory to the god of meekness, it's hard to keep your swagger. The temples fell into disrepair. The ash on the altars washed away. True, the planets still bear the Roman names, but how many of us notice them as we're taking our taxi down the esplanade? How many of us are certain that they are not merely stars?

The Problem with the Colosseum

Everyone wants it to continue—the arches, the latrines and animal cages, the rooms where men wept in what passed for their last privacy. When the emperor showed up, the lions ate the slaves. There could be no other outcome. It's still here at the center of Rome, obstructing traffic and collecting the dung of gulls. For the price of a shrimp dinner, we can see where Caesar sat. We can feel the stone that bore him up and which we have not let crumble.

Mutations and Duplications

These birds for example. So many songs and so few nests—they won't make sense until I find out where they came from. Isn't that always the case? Vestigial fingers show up inside the flipper of the whale, and "avocado" derives from the Aztec word for "testicle." Way leads on to way. I could trace myself back to an Irish king and still I'd have no idea. All the while, the swans are duplicating their grace in the waters of our lagoon.

Dung Beetle

Few people would interrogate you here. Nevertheless I take a stick and flip you onto your back. Your frantic legs look as though they're playing an invisible harp, and when I right you, you return to the feast that you alone enjoy. Later, at the cocktail party, my snooty neighbor is wearing a scarab brooch. She doesn't like it when I mention what you eat. No matter. The bright penny of your shell would be a pleasure in any setting. In this one, it is magnificent.

The Satin Lining of the Casket Reminds Me of a Jewelry Box

Consider the brooches of the dead, the wedding rings, the lockets full of faces. Assuming they don't get stolen by the men with shovels, such ornaments outlast everything. They are a kind of death tax, a toll on the way to oblivion. It isn't just jewelry. There are Bibles and flowers and lucky stuffed animals. We pack them in like we're burying pharaohs, like there's a pyramid of grief above them. And there is—only smaller, and made of dirt, in a land that won't stop raining.

Andromeda

We used to think it was a nebula, and there was a time when people didn't believe in germs. Of course, almost all the dishes ever made have broken, so what can we expect? Things transmute. Ptolemy misheard the sky above Egypt, and I was not the same person after leaning in to kiss you. This is what I've learned: The prettier the idea, the less likely it will last. The chain we forge is father to the rust.

Constellations

The stars of the flag are not the stars that matter. They have become a constellation that the wealthy use to navigate their yachts. When I step outside to show my daughters Sagittarius, the very center of our galaxy, they point only at the twinkling of passing jets. I need my neighbor to turn his floodlights off. I need the population to be less dense.

The Problem with Abundance

The Library of Congress started out with 740 books. Now there are 838 miles of filled shelves. At one time we could have contained what the library contained. Now we are awash in what we can never read. Sitting here on my bench, among the pigeons and the indigent, I feel like a monkey about to enter a freighter breaking apart on the American sandbar. It is packed to the ceiling with bananas and plums—the weatherman calling for flies.

Jonah

I could hear the gulls as the animal rose to taste the air, and I felt the plummeting after. Even then, it was clear the Lord had favored me. How else to explain that I sat in a soup that failed to digest me? After my disgorgement, the surf kept knocking me over as the beast tried to wriggle backward off the sandbar. The fist of its glassy eye refused to blink, and I thought the Lord was speaking to me through its wordless gaze. But then I saw the Ninevites, rushing down with their hunger and their knives. The gulls cried out and gathered, insisting that they share.

Pootatuck

It's the kind of river you can walk across. There is a fine scum tarnishing
every stone of it. Just look behind me. My steps are brightening the
sand, and because the river is clear and endless, the proof of my travels
speeds away. If I come back tomorrow, my path will have darkened, and
the water I walked through will be headed for the clouds. Somewhere a
child is looking up, guessing the animal my feet had been inside.

Sargasso

The seaweed collects and refuses to disperse—like moths around an August porchlight or the scent of dead raccoon. The message in a bottle goes undelivered here. Drowned bodies don't roll ashore. But now I learn the eel I caught in a Pennsylvania creek was born amid this tangle, that it likely was headed back that way after greasing my palms at twilight. I remember looking up, just after, how a jet slid over my portion of the sky like a cluster of noisy planets.

Essay on Memory

Most of our past has been forgotten—despite the pyramids and Anne
Frank's diary. Already Tuesday has all but disappeared. Sure, we
remember the traumas and the unexpected sex, but almost everything
else floats away like the weather inside this window. What's worse, in
those rare circumstances, when you and I recall the same moment,
they are as different as "shack" and "chalet." You bring up the bugs and
humidity, the scratches across your back. I recount how the bare branch
held your bra until we were ready to leave.

Whales

She tells me the ocean is full of whales. I've never felt the briny heat of their exhalations so it's something I take on faith, like the sturdiness of elevator cables, the existence of Ottawa. She is forever mentioning a largeness I have not seen—Niagara Falls, the Sears Tower, the sky above the prairie. She goes to these places to see for herself, and she tells me the story of a man she knew. He was at sea and saw spiders blowing on the wind without any land in sight. He was not a liar. He was looking for whales.

Seaplane

The seaplane circles the lake, checking for logs and swimmers. It is a further confirmation that we wish to go everywhere, unconstrained, like the smell of dead skunk on Sugar Street. Columbus didn't care if his inadvertent genocide came to define him. He was looking for pepper and cinnamon. The unaimed bullet goes on with its exploration. The avalanche speeds toward level ground.

Airport Finches

The finches inside the Frontier terminal have attained a kind of afterlife. While snow builds up on the tarmac, they enjoy a guilty warmth. Here they have learned to live without darkness. They have forgotten the taste of worms. Sometimes, as they flit from chair back to plastic plant, they think about the door that let them in—like a tear in the bag that shatters your wine and shows how the street is thirsty.

Less Buoyant

Yesterday, the meadow was full of daisies and black-eyed Susans. It looked like a million small balloons were pulling the whole place skyward. Now they are baling the meadow into tidy blocks the horses will eat all winter, ingesting a field that floated where now we see only tracks. This is always the case. The moon shows up like a cigarette hole, and the weather keeps milling our mountains into sand.

The Boundaries Are as Blurred as They've Ever Been

Think of the *Euglena*, the hermaphrodite, the foggy horizon above the sea. And then there's my microbiome, outnumbering my own cells by ten to one. Outside the window, a smashed possum becomes a strutting crow, the stink of it surrounding us. Ah, for the days of signatures and proofs, the cancer removed in a single lump. It is no longer possible to say where I end and it begins. We have had to make do without our glasses, and this is what I've seen: A dirt road followed long enough dissolves into trackless field, the buttercups lolling with the weight of bees, no matter how often I brush them away.

Baby Teeth

O misshapen pearls, O pebbles from the human brook, I summon the rusty taste of you, the pleasures of twisting. You were the first lesson in how nothing lasts, but no one paid attention. Pillow by pillow, we gathered your coins. Whatever we purchased is also gone.

Asymmetry

The lopsided tree eventually topples, and the fiddler crab must carry its heavy, unmusical claw. Consider the pinched eyes of the flounder, how it must live and die without seeing the mud it rides. The world is full of ill proportions—a lack of balance, of fairness. If I tore away this bedroom roof, you'd see how the stars have mostly brightened the sky above your side.

Peru Went to War over Guano

It still owns the Chincha Islands, taken because of excrement, stony layers of it that were sometimes 150 feet deep. Even today, guano is mined and ground up and taken by ship to the gardens and factories of America. What a world we live in. Shit is prized. It is both a consequence of hunger and a lesson in sustainable farming—fattening the tomato inside our sandwich like a bloody slice of moon.

Impotence

A wind clears out the last of the low-lying clouds. Here they are again—the unpressable buttons of the stars.

Paint

I pry up the bright coin of its lid and behold the destroyer of shirts, the speckler of grand pianos. True, I have turned the furniture to ghosts, and I have spread out *The New York Times* like a sidewalk along our walls. None of it matters. I should know by now that ruin has a way of finding us, that only my toe print on the bedroom floor can prove that we resisted.

Uncle Brian

Forty years ago, he gave me a piece of coral from the Philippines, where he'd met his first wife. She left him shortly thereafter, but I still have the coral. Bone white, the shape of an ear—it fits inside my fist. I doubt he remembered giving it to me, and because he died last Tuesday, I picked it from the little dish of keepsakes on our coffee table. Even the first wife made it to the funeral, but I stayed home and thought about coral—an animal whose skeleton is suited for display.

20 to 1

The last Neanderthals were 20 times older than the memory of Christ.
Uranus is 20 times farther from the Sun than the Earth, and yet we
can see it—if we know where to look, if we trust ourselves to pick it out
among the assembled faintness. It is the same ratio as when I was 40
and my daughter was 2. It's the difference between a full pack and your
last cigarette. Not much, is what I'm trying to say.

Evidence

On the map I have, the topographic lines of this hill look like God forgot to wipe away his fingerprint before he got in his Bible and fled. I knew one of the murdered boys. I had handed him a tissue once, to wipe his nose, as my daughter played piano at her recital. The apologists are full of mysterious ways, but I know evil when I see it. I can feel the thumb above me now, pressing down, fitting the grooves of this hillside.

Secret

Right now, for example, I'm walking down 5th Avenue and nobody knows that my socks don't match. One is a deep maroon, the other verging on teal. Oh sure, you could Smirnoff my evening, but still I wouldn't talk. Even a CAT scan produces only mumbles. My secret is like the daylight moon. It is easy to miss and it never lends you light. Remember this: No matter how close you get, you will never hear the song inside my head.

Ethanethiol

We spend our lives eradicating garlic from our breath and the cheesy smell of old shoes, but yours is an odor we cultivate. You keep us from arriving at smithereens, and you do not whisper as you step inside a room. Instead, you shout like a shelf of Calphalon hitting the kitchen tiles. Your intentions are good, though you can't help letting the suicide know that even her death will be unpleasant.

Argument

The clouds for me are the clouds for you. It doesn't matter what music is playing in your hotel room. We both have the same jar pressed over us. Birds are another matter. Last night I woke to moonlight and the purring of owls. Whatever their message, it was meant for me. Unmistakable— like a kiss or a middle finger. In the daylight, the branches above our bed were empty, and the traffic arose like a sonic fog, none of it coming closer.

Status Report

I was out in the yard standing where the grass butted up against the woods. A dog was barking on the farthest hill, and Venus hovered like a drill hole full of light. As often happens, some bats began looping the air above me as I thought about a girl I hadn't kissed enough. My family was on the inside. I saw them moving in the lighted squares—practicing algebra, removing mascara. It was like staring into a mortgaged aquarium, and I waited for one of them to wonder where I'd gone.

32 Stripes

The dent in my fingernail from where the hammer struck is moving, week by week, closer to being clipped. It used to take 36 stripes with the mower to clear the front yard; now it takes 32. I keep telling people the woods are trying to get inside our house, but I'm being dramatic. After all, the shrinking lawn is mostly due to my own laziness, my wish to see what the pokeweed looks like as the berries fill with ink. Still, Everest is rising 5 millimeters per year. It will eventually become unclimbable again—the bodies of the fallen preserved and carried into the speeding clouds.

Moon

The dirty monocle stares down at us. It is keeping the birds awake.
Somewhere, the tides are rising, drowning the shoreline stone by stone.
We cannot read by this light, we cannot discern the colors of our map.
Only worry thrives beneath this strange eye, and no matter how hard we
hurl these rocks, it will not look away.

Everybody Knows About the Other Two

But Michael Collins kept orbiting while the lunar module dropped like a spider to the bathroom floor. For 21 hours and 36 minutes, he was the loneliest man alive, and on the dark side, Collins lost contact with all but the pressurized stink of the capsule, the lights of his switches and dials. They became more important than the sky itself, blazing beyond his window. It must have been unnerving—the need to be touched, the need to not touch anything.

Frantic Counting

A bottle of champagne contains 250 million bubbles. I have no idea who came up with that number. I don't even believe it. The events surrounding an uncorking are not conducive to an accurate census: the proposal accepted, the baby arrived, the desperate new year underway at last. I admit it. I'm a sucker for the green glass of an opened bottle of Bollinger, the dense emerald of it, the sizzle in the flutes as we're peeling off our clothes. Don't talk to me of plans and future times. Let the frantic counting begin.

The Problem with Invention

Invention gives rise to invention. The blade demanded a handle; the ark unleashed a flood. It's always been like this. Luckily, under the right circumstances, a maple tree can become a violin. It allows us to utter Vivaldi, and someone is always waiting with a need we didn't know. You'd never guess there was a drought on this side of the dam. Listen, downriver, the sound of everyone you will never hear.

Inadvertent Mousetrap

The moon doesn't look different despite our having been there. That's the exception. Even the slopes of Everest are stained with urine and the bodies of fallen climbers. Just look at Brooklyn. It used to be farms, and before that, forests. Last November, I stood a bottle in the shed. By the time the lilacs had broken out, the bottle was full of dead mice in search of a tunnel that would take them to warmth. It's just another story, another attempt at tranquility, undone by our lightest touch.

Cold

The berries on the cedar tree turn purple and the waxwings descend. As for me, the early darkness disorients until the stars come on where they have always been. My neighbor's boat is back behind his house again, wrapped in plastic. Sometimes he forgets to turn his floodlights off, deterring prowlers but ruining the sky. At bedtime, we listen to the field mice finding the old ways back inside. My wife curls into me. Tomorrow, she says, we'll need to put out the traps.

That's Why I'm Headed to Greece

This is not the sky I would have chosen. The kitchen ran out of kokoretsi, and that tree doesn't go with this shirt. I guess the women had somewhere else to be. I guess the moon doesn't need directions. Come closer, I can't read the fine print without my other glasses. Asclepius is still waiting for his rooster, and the sun has risen to scant applause. Farewell, indigo petunias. I'm off to the land of Socrates and all that it entails.

The Problem with Putting "Audubon" in the Name of the Local Nature Center

Before he could paint the birds, he had to murder them. Everyone forgets that part.

Moon Monologue

The Smithsonian "touchrock" is a triangular slice of the moon collected in December 1972 during the Apollo 17 mission.

I regret the wedge made duller by the touch of a billion thumbs. It should be up here with me, riding the sky that suffocates, telling the Potomac to shimmer like dimes. Try to understand: There isn't a window I can't fit inside and the ocean crawls at my command. You should be more sympathetic. Half of me always endures a brightness not my own. Even as I wane to a pale sickle, the part of me you cannot see is a plate of baking bone.

Perspective

Yesterday at the museum I spent an hour among the coprolites. Some of them were cut apart and polished. They were pretty on the inside, flecked with amethyst and calcium. The little cards speculated on the animals that might have made them, but two things were certain: They were older than any religion; they would outlast any poem.

The Arms of the Venus de Milo

Just yesterday I was complaining about the lack of comets, and now I've found the arms of the Venus de Milo in a box at my neighbor's garage sale. Nothing stays missing forever. The skink's tail eventually grows back; someone picks up the dropped umbrella as soon as the rain begins. Even *The New York Times* agrees: A Copper Age hunter emerges from the glacier to show us his tattoos; a farmer in Michigan plows up a woolly mammoth and everyone wants a picture. Be patient. The world is working. The car keys you've been looking for are always where you left them.

Evolution

The ice used to be a mile thick above your house, and every now and then the river uncovers a shard of Colonial flatware, an arrowhead, a piece of beer bottle incapable of cutting anything. The fragments add up. They tell us the story of how nothing can stay the same. I no longer worry that caterpillars are destroying my only oak. I don't care if the Planning and Zoning Board approves another nail salon. Whenever you say that you'll never leave your husband, I remind myself that whales used to live on land, that they weren't much bigger than dogs.

Tetragrammaton

O unpronounceable name of the Lord, we have spent the centuries trying out ways to fit you inside our mouths. It hasn't worked, resulting in the Crusades, the burning of witches, the house arrest of Galileo. There can be no solution if we cannot name the problem, but let me say something anyway. When I see your four unspeakable consonants, I think of a nest with four different kinds of eggs in it. They don't make any sense together, but that doesn't stop the hatching.

The Problem with This Dirt

It's the kind of dirt you bury pets in. They always die when the ground is full of rocks, forcing you to purchase a pick as the hardware store is closing. At another time you might have grown a garden here. You're that dumb is what I'm saying. Look at all these trees; the rabbits breed unhindered. But go ahead. Stake up the tomato plants and wait for the fruit to stall. Keep on digging for as long as you like. Even after it's clear the coyotes cannot get him, the dog will not be deep enough.

A Pink Flame Rose out of It

The basement door has stopped closing with a click. The house is shifting. Soon our children won't need us anymore. The cactus was a good choice though. It doesn't mind when we forget to water it. One week, we both remembered, and then we remembered again. A pink flame rose out of it as if it were a candle. That surprised us. It illuminated nothing. In another time, we would have worried about the baby finding the basement stairs.

Hunger

The hawk is circling a sky the color of wet newspapers. All over town the goldenrod is going to seed, and the bees turn lazy with the lack of flowers. Even so the hunger persists. Look around. The nests in the trees are suddenly obvious. The sand confirms the animals. I think of you not thinking of me. I find the last good berry in the center of a bush. The hawk is farther off now, but the river keeps sliding through the middle of this field, draining a place that is somewhere full.

Candy

It was the first thing I stole. It was how I learned. Now the women in my office maintain little dishes of it beside their desks. They want me to eat it, and yet I wait until no one is looking. On my way back from the men's room, I remove what is best. I never refill. I suppress the crackling of cellophane.

Punishment

Everyone forgets that the devil's in hell too. He isn't a warden. He doesn't go home at the end of his shift. All the great punishments are permanent. Sisyphus has his boulder; Mariah Carey's lip syncing lives on in the ether of YouTube. It all makes sense. If you didn't get a scar from taking out the baked ziti with your bare hands, you'd reach in again next Sunday night.

The Quickness of Miracles Unbelieved

I look up and the clouds are sneaking away again. They are no better than foxes. Despite the thorns, the berries all go missing. Face it, the meteors are happening as we sleep, and the hummingbird won't wait until you grab a camera. Too slow, too slow—whatever spilled into our neighbor's trash is already back inside its hole.

Inventory

When the wind is right, I can hear the prison's PA system drifting out of the woods. There's a mouse nest inside the bluebird box. There's a broken chainsaw out in the shed. It's not all bad. We have three guitars, a full set of china without any chips, a leaking pipe that has somehow self-repaired. I love this family. The parakeets have their way with the financial section, and the mortgage continues without hope of commutation.

En Dash

I am a minus sign, a horizon of ink. I am a tabletop with the legs knocked out, a levitating dime in profile. I am the spine of a thin collection of poems. I am half of an equals sign, an underscore for emptiness. I am a pen full of love letters lying by the bed. Too long to be a hyphen, too short to cause a pause—I am a trapeze handle with no girl attached, a single rung on the ladder towards God, the sill of the window I'm standing on.

Dispatch

Nothing said asters like that meadow of dying bees. The honey was in the hive and headed for the jar. I tried not to think of its sweetness. The goal was always to eliminate goals: This was the teaching of the Buddha and of deadbeats everywhere. I thought back to a pond where the bottom was mostly beaver shit, how the long stems of water lilies rose up to my world, detonating among dragonflies and picnic music. The girls in their fraying shorts. Their lovely, precancerous tans.

Truth and Goodness and Beauty

The ancient Greeks had the right idea, but they've been dead for centuries. Sooner than not, we'll have to rely on what someone said that Plato said. It's happening even now. Think of Monet's *Water Lilies* succumbing in the fire of 1958. You can find pictures of it, but you'll never understand the texture of the paint. Alas, the unreadable world accumulates inside the sleekness of our phones. It won't be long before everything true is neither good nor beautiful.

The Smallest Russian Doll

I feel like the smallest Russian doll. This doesn't stop people from giving me a twist. I can hear them cursing as they search for my cocaine, the combination to the safe. Nobody wants to come across an irreducible kernel and find it wanting. Thus another woman has told me to take her back. Thus the moon like a dirty plate refuses both faucet and tongue.

The End of Mystery

Here, in the golden age of pornography, the full range of human pleasure and degradation fits inside our pockets. Year by year the stars get harder to see, and my cigarettes have blurred the once fine distinctions my tongue could make of your body. The answers exist, and Google is happy to find them for us. Someday soon, they tell me, a robot will be able to write this poem—only better, and in a font I can't imagine.

They Need Something More Durable
Than Longing and Wine

This is why lovers show off their dog bites and appendectomy scars, the tattooed crosses they have come to regret. They keep them hidden until they can't, until somebody touches with a tongue the place that used to hurt. After all this time, ink remains the medium of love letters. It's how the future knows what happened.

Acknowledgments

AMP: "Airport Finches";

Anthropocene: "Punishment," "The Boundaries Are as Blurred as They've Ever Been";

Arsenic Lobster: "The Satin Lining of the Casket Reminds Me of a Jewelry Box";

Barrow Street: "A River of Birds";

Belle Ombre: "Evolution," "That's Why I'm Headed to Greece";

Beloit Poetry Journal: "Moon";

Bookends Review: "Paint";

Breakwater: "Everybody Knows About the Other Two," "Peru Went to War Over Guano";

Connecticut River Review: "Candy";

Descant: "Evidence";

Diaphanous: "The Problem with Abundance";

Dusie: Tuesday Poem: "Whales";

Escape Into Life: "32 Stripes," "En Dash," "Essay on Memory," "Mutations and Duplications";

Gargoyle: "Perspective";

Hartford Courant: "Baby Teeth," "Greetings," "Marbles," "The Problem with Abundance," "The Roman Names";

Louisiana Literature: "The Problem with This Dirt";

North Dakota Quarterly: "The Smallest Russian Doll";

Oyster River Pages: "Less Buoyant";

Pidgeonholes: "Pootatuck," "Truth and Goodness and Beauty";

Pithead Chapel: "Status Report";

Plume: "Cold," "Uncle Brian";

Proem: "Argument";

Prose Poetry: An Introduction (Princeton University Press): "The Pond";

Rhino: "Asymmetry";

Salamander: "Andromeda";

82: "Inventory," "The Quickness of Miracles Unbelieved";

The Cincinnati Review: "Greetings," "Hunger";

The Gettysburg Review: "Jonah," "The End of Mystery," "The Problem
    with the Colosseum";
The New Yorker: "The Pond";
The Night Heron Barks: "Sargasso";
The Racket: "The Problem with Invention";
The Southern Review: "Frantic Counting," "Inadvertent Mousetrap,"
    "Marbles," "Moon Monologue," "The Roman Names";
The Wax Paper: "20 to 1," "Dispatch";
Third Point Press: "A Pink Flame Rose out of It";
Tulane Review: "Everybody Knows About the Other Two," "Impotence,"
    "Peru Went to War over Guano," "Tetragrammaton";
Unbroken Journal: "Baby Teeth," "They Need Something More Durable
    Than Longing and Wine";
*Waking Up to the Earth: Connecticut Poets in a Time of Global Climate
    Crisis* (Grayson Books): "Seaplane";
West Trade Review: "Constellations," "The Arms of the Venus de Milo."

Some of these poems appeared in the chapbook *The Problem with
Abundance* (Grayson Books, 2019).

Many thanks, as always, for BJ Ward's close attention to these poems. I
can't finish anything without him.

About the Author

Charles Rafferty is the author of eight chapbooks and six full-length collections of poetry, most recently *The Smoke of Horses* (BOA Editions, 2017). His poems have appeared in *The New Yorker; O, The Oprah Magazine; The Southern Review; The Cincinnati Review; Prairie Schooner; Salamander; Rhino; The Gettysburg Review;* and *Ploughshares.* He is also the author of two collections of short fiction, most recently *Somebody Who Knows Somebody* (Gold Wake Press, 2021). His first novel, *Moscodelphia,* is forthcoming from Woodhall Press. He has won grants from the National Endowment for the Arts and the Connecticut Commission on Culture and Tourism. Currently, he co-directs the MFA program at Albertus Magnus College and teaches at the Westport Writers' Workshop. He lives in Connecticut with his wife, two daughters, one dog, and four parakeets. He is especially interested in local archaeology, mushroom identification, and swamp ecology.

BOA Editions, Ltd., American Poets Continuum Series

Colophon

BOA Editions, Ltd., a not-for-profit publisher of poetry and other literary works, fosters readership and appreciation of contemporary literature. By identifying, cultivating, and publishing both new and established poets and selecting authors of unique literary talent, BOA brings high-quality literature to the public. Support for this effort comes from the sale of its publications, grant funding, and private donations.

The publication of this book is made possible, in part, by the support of the following individuals:

Anonymous (x3)

Nelson Adrian Blish

Gary & Gwen Conners

Charles & Danielle Coté

The Chris Dahl & Ruth Rowse Charitable Fund

Bonnie Garner

Robert L. Giron

Margaret Heminway

Kathleen C. Holcombe

Nora A. Jones

Paul LaFerriere & Dorrie Parini

Marcia Lowry

Joe McElveney

Sherry Phillips & Richard Margolis Donor Advised Fund

Boo Poulin

Deborah Ronnen

Thomas Smith & Louise Spinelli

Elizabeth Spenst

Sue S. Stewart, *in memory of Steven L. Raymond*

William Waddell & Linda Rubel

Michael Waters & Mihaela Moscaliuc

Bruce & Jean Weigl